SPIES and LIES—
Famous and Infamous SPIES

BY SUSAN K. MITCHELL

THE SECRET WORLD OF S

Enslow Publishers, Inc.
40 Industrial Road
Box 398
Berkeley Heights, NJ 07922
http://www.enslow.com

For my wonderful parents, Robbie & Dub

Library of Congress Cataloging-in-Publication Data

Mitchell, Susan K.
    Spies and lies : famous and infamous spies / Susan K. Mitchell.
        p. cm. — (The secret world of spies)
    Includes index.
    Summary: "Explores famous and infamous spies in history, including examples of female spies,
        child spies, family spy rings, and animal spies"—Provided by publisher.
    ISBN 978-0-7660-3713-7
    1. Espionage—Juvenile literature. 2. Spies—Juvenile literature. I. Title.
    UB270.5.M576 2012
    327.12092'2—dc22

                                                    2010044126

Paperback ISBN 978-1-59845-349-2

Printed in China

052011 Leo Paper Group, Heshan City, Guangdong, China

10 9 8 7 6 5 4 3 2 1

To Our Readers: We have done our best to make sure all Internet addresses in this book
were active and appropriate when we went to press. However, the author and the publisher
have no control over and assume no liability for the material available on those Internet
sites or on other Web sites they may link to. Any comments or suggestions can be sent by
e-mail to comments@enslow.com or to the address on the back cover.

Illustration Credits: AP Images, pp. 30, 34; AP Images / Diether Endlicher, p. 27; Federal
Bureau of Investigation (FBI), p. 17; Getty Images, p. 41; The Granger Collection, New
York, pp. 9, 10, 25; Courtesy of the International Spy Museum, p. 33; Library of Congress,
pp. 7, 12; Rue des Archives / The Granger Collection, New York, p. 40; Shutterstock
.com, pp. 3, 4, 18, 26, 39, 42, 44; United States Holocaust Memorial Museum (USHMM),
courtesy of Charles Martin Roman, p. 24; USHMM, courtesy of National Archives and
Records Administration, p. 15; U.S. Navy, pp. 19, 38.

Cover Illustration: Mehau Kulyk / Photo Researchers, Inc. (background); Shutterstock.com
(spy silhouette image, lower right corner).

CONTENTS

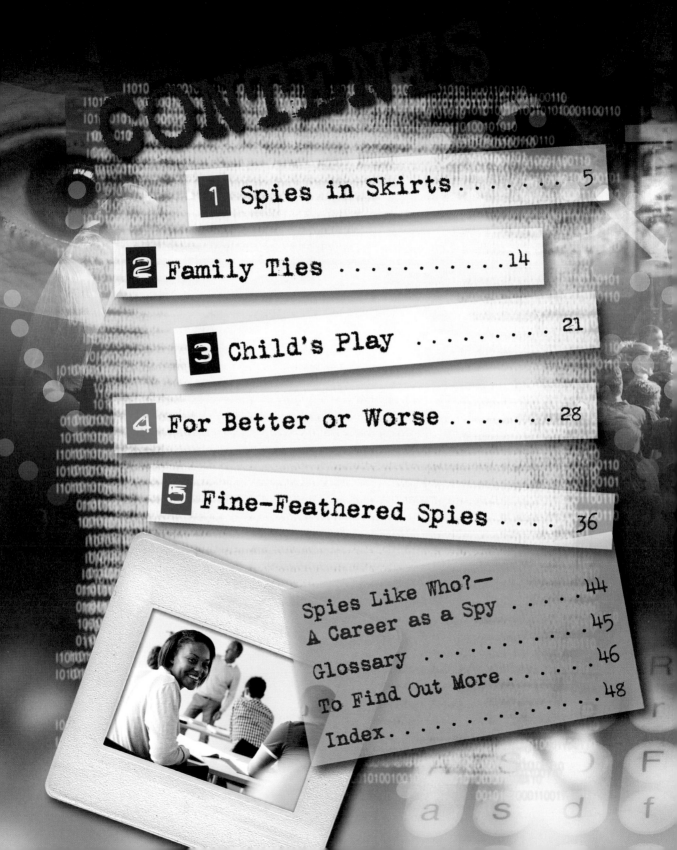

Chapter 1

Spies in Skirts

The best spies are those who are never suspected. It is true that most spies in history have been men. However, there are many successful spies who never fit that category. Women, children, and even animals have been spies as well. They were able to spy because few enemies expected them to actually be spies. Throughout history, women and children have been considered less important than men.

They often held less visible places in society. It is that same treatment that could also make them perfect spies. That is especially true for women.

Using female spies goes back hundreds of years. It even dates as far back as the American Revolution and the Civil War. These women were often the unsung heroes of the wars. They risked their lives for their beliefs. Few of them have more than a side note in history, however.

Perilous Petticoats

One of the most famous female Civil War spies was Belle Boyd. She was just seventeen years old when she began her career as a bold spy for the South. In her childhood, Belle had been a bit of a tomboy. She was always drawn to adventure. She seemed suited for spying. Boyd was also quite a flirt. She used every ounce of her feminine charm in her career as a spy.

This charm helped Boyd get out of trouble more than once. She was reported as a spy several times. She was arrested at least six times. Boyd even went to prison more than once. Each time, she batted her eyelashes. She turned on the tears. Boyd was released every time.

Belle Boyd was a spy for the South during the Civil War. This photo of her was taken sometime between 1855 and 1865.

Boyd was not just interested in the romance of spying. She loved the South with great passion. She would do anything to help the South in the Civil War. She proved her bravery in May 1862. Belle got word that Southern general Thomas "Stonewall" Jackson's troops were headed her way.

Spies for the Blue and the Gray

The Civil War was a bitter battle in U.S. history. Northern states fought Southern states and both sides used spies. Sometimes, those spies were women. During the Civil War, the South was not the only side with a famous female spy. The North had Elizabeth Van Lew. She was an even more successful spy than Belle Boyd. Van Lew managed to sneak information out of Southern president Jefferson Davis's own home!

At one point during her spy career, Van Lew stopped combing her hair. She dressed in tattered clothes. She also walked around mumbling to herself. This behavior earned her the nickname "Crazy Bet." Van Lew was no crazy woman, however. This was just a clever disguise.

Elizabeth Van Lew carried this cipher code in her watch case until her death in 1900. She used the cipher to help spy for the Union army.

Belle Boyd was a bit of a celebrity in Europe. The French newspapers called her "La Belle Rebelle"—or Belle the Rebel.

The Belle of the Battlefield

Northern forces were already encamped in her town as Jackson and his men approached. Boyd had potentially valuable information on the enemy troops' numbers, locations, and plans. She hoped

Belle Boyd completed many spy missions for the South. Here she is doing spy work in the Union army prison for captured Southern soldiers at Manassas Junction, Virginia.

her information would help Jackson in battle. Boyd dashed into the streets. She begged some of the men to take the news to the general. None would agree to risk their lives.

Boyd knew it was up to her. By then, Northern forces had already begun to fire on the advancing South. Boyd grabbed her bonnet and raced across the battlefield. She waved her bonnet wildly in the air as a signal to the South. Enemy bullets sailed by Boyd. They were close enough to put bullet holes in her skirt. At one point, she had to dive on the ground before an enemy cannonball exploded right in front of her.

The sight of a woman sprinting across the battle-field amazed the Southern troops. Boyd was able to get the information about the small Northern troops to General Jackson. Jackson's soldiers won the battle.

Boyd was a heroine! She was awarded the Southern Cross of Honor. Her bravery impressed General Jackson, and he made her an honorary captain. Her spying days for the South ended, and she eventually fled to England. Her adventures, however, were not over. She traveled the world telling stories of her life as a famous spy.

General Thomas "Stonewall" Jackson, shown here on horseback, awarded Belle Boyd the Southern Cross of Honor for her heroic spy work during the Civil War.

SECRET FACT

During World War II, a female spy's most valuable possession might have been her stockings! Silk was very rare at the time. Her stockings could be used as a bribe to get out of trouble with the enemy.

Starstruck Spying

Famous spies were sometimes famous people. Some of them were truly spies. Others simply helped the Office of Strategic Services (OSS), a spy agency, in other ways. Jazz musician Josephine Baker was also a spy. She smuggled coded messages on her sheet music during World War II.

Famous chef Julia Child helped the OSS in research and development. She helped develop a shark repellent to assist navy divers.

Actress Marlene Dietrich recorded songs for the OSS. Some songs were anti-Nazi, and others were sad. One popular song, "Lili Marlene," was about leaving behind a sweetheart or loved one. These songs were broadcast to German troops. The hope was that it would lower the German troops' morale. The plan proved to be successful.

Family Ties

The family that spies together stays together. Unless, that is, they get caught. It is actually rare to find an entire family of spies in history. One that stands out, however, is the Kuehn family. In this family of four, everyone had a role to play. Even the children were part of the deception.

Bernard Kuehn was a German Nazi. He was friends with officials in the secret police in Germany. His older daughter, Susie Ruth, had dated a high-ranking Nazi.

His name was Joseph Goebbels. The Japanese asked the Nazis to recommend someone to spy on the United States.

Goebbels offered the job to Susie Ruth and her family. It was just what her father, Bernard, had hoped for. They were told to spy on the U.S. forces at Pearl Harbor in Hawaii. In August 1935, they set up their lives as a typical American family. Nothing was what it seemed.

Joseph Goebbels offered the Kuehn family the job of spying on the U.S. military at Pearl Harbor. In this photo, Goebbels speaks to a crowd of loyal Nazis on May 10, 1933.

All in the Family

Everyone in the Kuehn family had a role to play. Susie Ruth flirted with many of the U.S. sailors. She tried to gather as much information as she could. She also opened a local beauty salon near Pearl Harbor. Susie and her mother, Friedel, listened to the gossip of the military wives and girlfriends.

Friedel's job was to record everything the family found out. She traveled back and forth to Japan to pass along information. Friedel also brought back large sums of money. The Japanese paid the Kuehn family quite well for their spy work.

Even ten-year-old Hans Kuehn helped out in the act. Friedel would dress him in little sailor suits. She would walk Hans near the docks. Sailors thought the young boy was adorable. They offered to give him tours of the ships. Hans had been trained to notice everything. He would then tell his father every detail from the ships.

SINS of the Father

The Walker family spy ring was a father and son operation. John Walker, Jr., had been selling U.S. secrets to the Russians for many years. He was a former U.S. naval officer. Walker began spying for the Russians in 1967.

Eventually, his son, Michael, joined him. His son was also in the navy. He was the source of many of the military documents that Walker sold to the Russians. Even John Walker's brother, Arthur, was part of the family spy ring. Eventually, Walker's ex-wife tipped off the FBI. They were exposed and arrested in 1985.

This is John Walker's passport. The FBI took it from him after his arrest in 1985.

Over in a Flash

Bernard Kuehn kept track of every secret detail. He would flash coded messages from his attic window. He was communicating with the Japanese Embassy nearby. Every secret he passed along got the Japanese one step closer to an attack on the United States. Pearl Harbor was in danger.

Ultimately, it was the flashing coded messages that destroyed the Kuehn family. The U.S. military noticed the flashes coming from the Kuehn home. It was too late, however. The Japanese attacked Pearl Harbor on December 7, 1941. The attack was made so much easier because of the information the Kuehn family gave Japan.

The Kuehns used high-powered binoculars to spy on American ships.

SECRET FACT

Mr. and Mrs. Kuehn would often go on "research expeditions" around the island. They claimed they were studying Hawaiian land and life. In reality, they were watching ships through high-powered binoculars.

The Japanese attacked Pearl Harbor on December 7, 1941. The information the Kuehn family had gathered helped the Japanese plan their attack.

The flashing was enough, however, for the FBI to make an arrest. They began to investigate. Soon, they found out the extent of the Kuehn family's spying. Bernard Kuehn, his wife, and daughter were all arrested. All but Hans served time in jail. Bernard offered to trade information on the Japanese and the Nazis in order to escape execution. Instead, he was sentenced to fifty years in prison. After the war, he was sent back to Germany. His wife and daughter were sent back as well. The family that had spied together was punished together as well.

Sister Act

Sisters Ginnie and Lottie Moon were successful spies during the Civil War. They were masters at creating undercover identities to travel from place to place. Lottie often disguised herself as an old woman. Other times, she used false papers to claim she was a British citizen. She used each story so that she could pass along information for the South without being caught.

Ginnie would also come up with stories about who she was. At times, she claimed to be visiting relatives in a certain area. Her mother would even come with her. This made them look less suspicious to the Northern soldiers.

Child's Play

The very best spy is one that no enemy would ever suspect. Certainly, few enemies would expect a pint-size child to be a spy. Many times in history, this made it easier to overlook children as possible spies. Though using children as spies has never been an ordinary practice, it has happened in history.

Young to teen-aged children could move from place to place fairly easily. They are less likely to be searched by guards. It may be easy for them to carry information without being caught. The fact is that young people would not attract as much attention. They could often listen to conversations without being noticed.

One such spy was teenager Agnes Daluge. After many long illnesses as a child, Agnes moved to Germany to live with her aunt Rosa. She was only eleven years old at the time. World War II was raging and Rosa hated the Nazis. There was much more going on in her aunt's home than Agnes could have imagined.

One of the youngest spies in history is Ariel Bradley. He was only nine years old when he became a spy for George Washington!

Coming of Age as a Spy

Agnes's aunt was helping people escape the Nazis. Many of them were Jewish. During World War II, millions of Jewish people were killed or imprisoned by the Nazis. Helping them escape was a dangerous business. Anyone caught helping Jews could face the same fate from the Nazis. By the time Agnes was thirteen, she was swept up in the danger of her aunt's secret world. She became a spy for the Allied forces against the Nazis.

She quickly became successful at spying. Agnes was very small for her age. Years of illness had stunted her growth. However, she learned to use this to her advantage. Agnes used her small size as part of her disguise. She would often claim to be a much younger child.

Agnes pretended to be a child of escaping Jewish adults. Agnes and the Jewish adults would pretend to be a non-Jewish family to escape the Nazis. Agnes helped the family leave Germany and cross into Switzerland. Once the people were safely across the Swiss border, Agnes would sneak back into Germany again to help more people escape.

A Jewish family escapes Nazi capture by crossing the Alps mountains into Italy. Agnes Daluge helped many Jews escape the Nazis by guiding them into Switzerland.

Teenage Bravery

Trained by her aunt, Agnes learned many tricks of the spy trade. Her aunt Rosa urged Agnes to learn other languages. This helped Agnes when she was undercover. It gave her the ability to talk her way out of dangerous situations.

At one point, a German soldier held Agnes at knifepoint. A curfew was in place. People were not allowed to be outside after a certain time. Agnes was caught in the streets after hours. She used her childlike charm to talk her way out of trouble. The soldier let her go.

Agnes used her bravery to save more than Jewish people. She saved Allied soldiers as well. Once, she

Luck of the Dicey

During the American Revolution, Dicey Langston was one brave fifteen-year-old. She heard that a band of men loyal to the British were going to attack a patriot settlement in South Carolina. Dicey knew her brothers were there and that they were in danger. She decided to risk her life to warn them. Her message reached them just in time. By the time the loyalists arrived, the patriots—including Dicey's brothers—had escaped.

On another occasion, the same band of loyalists broke into the Langston home. They wanted to kill her father and brothers. Dicey stepped in front of her father. She stood between him and the soldier's rifle. The soldier was amazed. He agreed to let them go.

Dicey Langston protects her elderly father from loyalist troops during the American Revolution. Dicey risked her life on more than one occasion to save her family.

rushcd up the side of a hill near her aunt's home. She scrambled to reach a crashed U.S. military pilot before the Nazis could reach him. Agnes arrived first and got the pilot to safety.

After World War II, Agnes went back to a normal life. She married an American soldier and moved to the United States. For many years, not even her children knew of her exciting life. She told them nothing more than she had been a spy as a child. It was not until very late in life that they learned about her brave and dangerous work.

SECRET FACT

Agnes was also skilled at passing secret messages. She would play her accordion and nod or signal to certain parts in the music. These were really secret coded messages.

Agnes Daluge used an accordion to help pass secret messages through music.

Forced to Spy

Romanian leader Nicolae Ceausescu addresses a crowd during a speech on November 24, 1989, the same year he was executed. The Romanian leader created a child spy network during his rule.

During the Cold War, Romanian ruler Nicolae Ceausescu (NEE-co-lie show-SHES-coo) recruited more than one hundred teenage spies. He created networks of spies all over the country. Many of them were no older than twelve to fourteen years old.

The children were forced to work as spies. They were threatened and blackmailed. These young spies had to gather information on family members. They also had to spy on teachers and other adults near them. Ceausescu was removed from power and executed in 1989. However, only as recently as 2004 was the child spy network discovered.

Chapter 4

For Better or Worse

When a couple marries, they agree to work together through everything. For some couples, this even means spying together! It may also mean committing treason. That was the case for Julius and Ethel Rosenberg. They are one of the most infamous spy couples in history.

The young Jewish couple met in New York. Both were intelligent and passionate in their beliefs. Ethel worked as a secretary for a shipping company. Julius graduated college with a degree in electrical engineering. They were also both active communists. Both were members of the Youth Communist League. Beliefs such as these were very different from beliefs in American capitalism.

In 1939, Julius and Ethel married. Soon, Julius was working for the Army Signal Corps as a radar specialist. The young couple had also increased their activity in communism. They both became members of the American Communist Party. They began to attract the attention of the Soviet KGB.

SECRET FACT

At one point in his life, Julius studied to become a rabbi. Ethel had dreamed of becoming a singer.

House of Spies

The KGB contacted Julius Rosenberg in 1942. They recruited him to spy on America for them. It meant betraying his country. Julius did not hesitate. His beliefs in communism were stronger than anything else. He agreed to become a spy.

Julius (left) and Ethel Rosenberg began to attract attention from the Soviet KGB in 1939.

Julius had access to certain military information. His job with the Army Signal Corps was to inspect electronics made for the military. He passed along this information to the Soviets. Julius even stole a device built to bring down enemy airplanes. He turned this over to the KGB, too.

Soon, Julius involved more family members in his spy activities. Ethel's brother, David, worked at a military base called Los Alamos in New Mexico. This was where the atomic bomb was created. Julius convinced David to steal information on the bomb. They gave all the stolen information to the Soviets. Even Ethel's sister-in-law, Ruth, was involved. She was often in charge of carrying messages to the Soviet KGB.

'Til Death Do Us Part

The pressure of spy work soon became too much for David and Ruth to handle. By 1950, the FBI had figured out David's involvement. They confronted him with all they had learned. David agreed to tell them everything. That meant telling the FBI about Julius and Ethel.

There was much evidence that pointed to the spy work of Julius. Ethel's involvement was a bit more unknown. Both David and Ruth claimed that Ethel had been the one to type up the notes on Los Alamos. These were the notes passed along to the Soviets. At the very least, they claimed Ethel knew about her husband's role as a spy.

Spy Disguises

Tony and Jonna Mendez each had more than twenty years of experience with the Central Intelligence Agency (CIA) before they retired. The married couple each had exciting spy operations throughout their careers. They are best known, however, for their work creating disguises for the CIA.

Both Tony and Jonna served as the CIA's Chief of Disguises. It was their job to create believable disguises for spies undercover. Tony's background as an artist helped him come up with disguises so good even family members would not recognize the spy. Jonna's experience with photography helped her, too. In addition to working on disguises, she also worked with spy cameras.

Tony and Jonna Mendez created disguises for the CIA. The married couple also created these disguises for a staff member at the International Spy Museum. Can you recognize the woman once she is disguised?

The Rosenbergs stood trial in 1951. They were both found guilty and sentenced to death. Julius and Ethel claimed their innocence. They both were sent to jail to await their punishment. In 1953, the couple was executed. They were the first American civilian spies to be executed.

A view of the heavily guarded Los Alamos, New Mexico, military base. This is where the atomic bomb was created. Julius Rosenberg convinced his brother-in-law, David, to steal secrets about the bomb for the Soviets.

Ethel's brother, David, said years later that he lied about Ethel's involvement as a spy. He claimed he only lied to save his own wife, Ruth.

SECRET FACT

Spying by the Numbers

Agent 202 and Agent 123 worked for more than thirty years as spies for Cuba. Behind the numbers, however, was an American couple. Their names were Kendall and Gwendolyn Myers. They were supportive of Cuba and its dictator, Fidel Castro.

Their spy career began in 1981, fueled by a hatred of the United States. Kendall used his position in the State Department to gather secrets. He had access to high-level secret documents. The couple would then pass them along to the Cuban government. Their years of spying were over in 2009. The FBI arrested them.

Chapter 5

Fine-Feathered Spies

A spy can be anywhere. The cat rubbing against a park bench? The bird outside a window? Even these could be spies. It may sound crazy, but animal spies are very real. Of course, these animals have no idea they are being used as spies. They are merely tools in the human spy's kit.

Many different animals have been used as spies over the years. The military and intelligence agencies are always trying new ideas.

One of the oldest uses goes all the way back to ancient times. It is the use of homing pigeons. As far back as ancient Egypt, these birds were used to carry messages. Even Julius Caesar, the famous Roman leader, used them to carry secret messages.

Homing pigeons can travel very high above the enemy. They can also find their way back home. Most of all, the pigeons are easily ignored and overlooked. The enemy is not likely to pay attention to birds flying overhead. This made them a valuable spy tool during World War I.

SECRET FACT

Animal spies can even be underwater! Dolphins wearing special cameras have been trained to patrol military harbors. They can also be trained to capture photos of enemy ships.

Dolphins wearing special cameras can be trained to perform underwater surveillance.

Those Spies are Nuts!

Animal spies work for praise not pay. A few that were recently discovered apparently work for nothing more than nuts. In 2007, Iran claimed they found several spy squirrels near their border. Iranian newspapers even claim the squirrels were "arrested."

The newspapers said that the fourteen squirrels were equipped with high-tech listening devices. No one has been able to prove that these squirrels were spies. In fact, most scientists doubt squirrels could be used as spies.

Spies in the Sky

Homing pigeons were not only useful in carrying messages. They could also be trained to "take" pictures over enemy territory. The military would attach special small cameras to the pigeons. They would then fly over the enemy. The cameras were programmed to take pictures at certain intervals.

The pigeons returned home to their handlers. The camera they carried would have very important pictures about the location of enemy forces.

French soldiers release homing pigeons during World War I. Homing pigeons have been valuable spies throughout the ages.

A replica of Cher Ami, a homing pigeon used by the U.S. Army Signal Corps during World War I, is on display at the International Spy Museum. This winged spy was awarded the Croix de Guerre, a French military honor, for heroic service during battle.

The homing pigeons were very successful. During World War I, the U.S. Army reported that over 90 percent of messages sent by pigeon arrived safely.

Using pigeons as spies in World War I was so successful, they were used during World War II as well. These birds often flew missions during combat.

Some of them were wounded in battle. Several of the winged spies were awarded military honors.

Today, the role of pigeons in espionage is unknown. The CIA Museum has a battery-operated pigeon camera on display. The use of it, however, is still listed as classified and top secret.

Birds, Mice, and Cats—Oh My!

Pigeons are not the only animal spies used by intelligence agencies. One unsuccessful animal spy operation was Acoustic Kitty. In 1961, the CIA implanted a house cat with a listening device. The idea was to have the cat get close to a person they wanted to eavesdrop on.

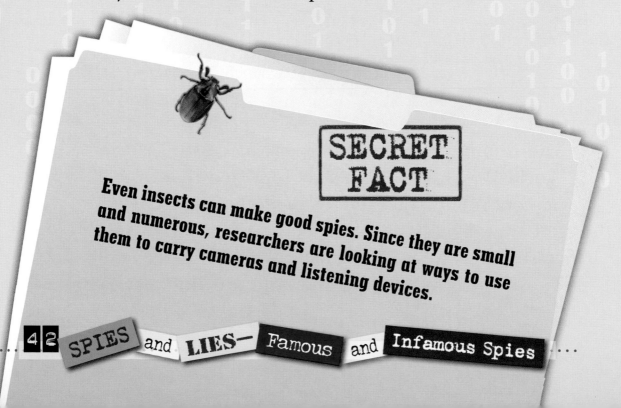

SECRET FACT

Even insects can make good spies. Since they are small and numerous, researchers are looking at ways to use them to carry cameras and listening devices.

Unfortunately, it is difficult to make a cat go where you want. The Acoustic Kitty wandered everywhere but where the CIA wanted her to go. The CIA removed the listening device from the cat. The spy project was abandoned. Acoustic Kitty went back to her life as a regular cat.

The project taught the spy agencies that it is best to use animals that are more easily trained. In Britain, the MI6 decided to use mice. Mice may be small, but they can be trained. They used a mouse to deliver a listening device into the home of a suspected spy. The tiny mouse could fit through small spaces in the home without being seen. These and other animals prove that you do not have to have wings to make a great spy.

Suspect the Unsuspected

It is true that spies can be anyone and anywhere. They are most effective when they are the least obvious. The people who society tends to overlook often make the most successful spies. Children, women, families, and even animals can go without notice. All the while, they may be listening and gathering information.

SPIES

Like

Who?

A CAREER AS A SPY

Working as a spy for the CIA is no easy job to get. The actual title of the spy department is the Clandestine Services. Field agents are called core collectors. They are usually between twenty-five and thirty-five years old. The CIA requires at least a bachelor's degree with a minimum of a 3.0 grade average.

Foreign travel and experience is a bonus. Knowing how to speak languages other than English is also highly valued in a core collector. Hopeful agents must have good communication skills. The ability to write clearly and accurately is important. Agents go through a training program. They can expect to make between $50,000 and $70,000 per year.

Would you like to get a job as a spy for the CIA? You must earn a college degree first. Fluency in languages other than English is a plus. Eventually you must go through a training program before acceptance into the Clandestine Services.

Glossary

acoustic—Pertaining to the sense of hearing.

Allied forces—The countries that fought on the side of the United States during World War II.

betraying—To turn against one's country.

blackmailed—To force a person to do something by using threats or intimidation.

capitalism—An economic system in which the means of production and distribution are privately owned and operated for profit.

combat—During war, armed fighting with enemy forces.

communism—A political system where the government owns most economic resources and divides them among the citizens.

dictator—A person in charge who has absolute power.

embassy—The official headquarters for a country's ambassador or representative.

loyalists—During the American Revolution, a term to describe those loyal to Britain.

To Find Out More

Books

Burgan, Michael. **Spies and Traitors: Stories of Masters of Deception.** Mankato, Minn.: Capstone Press, 2010.

Coleman, Janet Wyman. **Secrets, Lies, Gizmos, and Spies: A History of Spies and Espionage.** New York: Harry N. Abrams, 2006.

Denega, Danielle. **The Cold War Pigeon Patrols and Other Animal Spies.** New York: Franklin Watts, 2008.

Head, Honor. **Famous Spies.** Mankato, Minn.: Smart Apple Media, 2010.

O'Shei, Tim. **Cold War Spies.** Mankato, Minn.: Capstone Press, 2008.

Wagner, Heather Lehr. **Spies in the Civil War.** New York: Chelsea House Publishers, 2009.

Internet Addresses

Central Intelligence Agency (CIA):
  Kids' Page

  <https://www.cia.gov/kids-page/index.html>

International Spy Museum for Kids

  <http://www.spymuseum.org/kids>

U.S. Department of Defense: "Civil War
  Spies: Good Intell Knows No Gender"

  <http://www.defense.gov/news/newsarticle
    .aspx?id=45683>

Index